MARTIN VAN BUREN

OUR EIGHTH PRESIDENT

by Steven Ferry

THE CHILD'S WORLD ®

PUBLISHED IN THE UNITED STATES OF AMERICA

THE CHILD'S WORLD®
1980 Lookout Drive • Mankato, MN 56003-1705
800-599-READ • www.childsworld.com

ACKNOWLEDGMENTS
The Child's World®: Mary Berendes, Publishing Director

Creative Spark: Mary McGavic, Project Director; Melissa McDaniel, Editorial
Director; Deborah Goodsite, Photo Research

The Design Lab: Kathleen Petelinsek, Design; Gregory Lindholm, Page Production

Content Adviser: David R. Smith, Adjunct Assistant Professor of History,
University of Michigan, Ann Arbor

PHOTOS
Cover and page 3: White House Historical Association (White House Collection)
(40), detail. White House Historical Association (White House Collection) (40)

Interior: Alamy: 11, 13 (North Wind Picture Archives), 35 (David Caton);
The Art Archive: 10, 31 and 39 (Culver Pictures); The Bridgeman Art Library
International: 15, 30 (Collection of the New-York Historical Society, USA),
19 (Private Collection, Photo © Christie's Images), 36 (Private Collection,
Ken Welsh); Corbis: 4 and 38 (Francis G. Mayer), 21 bottom and 38, 25
(Bettmann); Getty Images: 21 top (Kean Collection/Archive Photos), 29; The
Granger Collection, New York: 5, 7, 8, 9, 14, 18, 20, 22, 23 and 39, 24, 27, 32;
Independence National Historical Park: 6 (National Park Service. Independence
National Historical Park Archives); iStockphoto: 44 (Tim Fan); The Library
of Congress Collection: 17, 33, 37; Photolibrary.com: 34 (Salvatore Vasapolli/
Animals Animals/Earth Scenes); U.S. Air Force photo: 45; White House Historical
Association: 12, (White House Collection), detail, 28, (White House Collection),
detail.

LIBRARY OF CONGRESS CATALOGING-IN-PUBLICATION DATA
Ferry, Steven, 1953–
  Martin Van Buren / by Steven Ferry.
    p. cm. — (Presidents of the U.S.A.)
  Includes bibliographical references and index.
  ISBN 978-1-60253-037-9 (library bound : alk. paper)
1. Van Buren, Martin, 1782–1862—Juvenile literature. 2. Presidents—United
States—Biography—Juvenile literature. I. Title. II. Series.

E387.F46 2008
973.5'7092—dc22
  [B]
                                          2007049061

Martin Van Buren
served as president
from 1837 to 1841.

TABLE OF CONTENTS

chapter one
THE YOUNG POLITICIAN   4

chapter two
THE RED FOX OF KINDERHOOK   12

chapter three
THE CAREFUL DUTCHMAN   22

chapter four
STANDING FIRM   31

Time Line   38

Glossary   40

The United States Government   42

Choosing the President   43

The White House   44

Presidential Perks   45

Facts   46

For More Information   47

Index   48

THE YOUNG POLITICIAN

In 1782, the United States had just won the Revolutionary War. That same year, future president Martin Van Buren was born on December 5 in Kinderhook, New York. He was the third of Abraham and Maria Van Buren's eight children. The Van Buren family had farmed in the Hudson Valley for 150 years before Abraham Van Buren turned their farmhouse into a tavern. He was also involved in Kinderhook's government. The town often used his tavern as a **polling place** for state and national elections.

*Martin Van Buren
as a young man*

Kinderhook is a small town on the eastern shore of the Hudson River. In Van Buren's day, it was populated mainly by people of Dutch descent. At that time, Kinderhook was the center of life between the cities of Albany and Poughkeepsie. It was also a stopping point for people traveling from New York

City to Albany, the capital of New York. Many lawyers and politicians visited Abraham Van Buren's tavern to drink and discuss **politics.** Van Buren supported Thomas Jefferson's **political party,** the Democratic-Republicans, but he was careful to remain **neutral** in these discussions. He did not want to have disagreements with his customers. Perhaps it was due to his father's influence that Martin Van Buren never lost his temper in public.

Little Mat, as people called Martin, grew up in a Dutch-speaking household. He worked as a delivery boy from a young age. He pulled a heavy sled of groceries through the snow, making deliveries to people around town. Afterward, he would rush home to help

Martin Van Buren was born in this house in Kinderhook. His family had farmed the surrounding land for 150 years.

Martin Van Buren supported the ideas of Thomas Jefferson. He wanted to limit the power of the federal government and defend personal liberties.

Martin Van Buren was the first American president born after the United States declared its independence.

Kinderhook means "Children's Corner" in Dutch.

The Van Burens owned six slaves while Martin was growing up. As an adult, Martin Van Buren kept one slave, Tom, for many years.

at the family tavern. There he would listen carefully to the discussions, noting how his father always listened but said little. His father believed in Thomas Jefferson's **principles** of a limited national government. Jefferson believed that the states should have more power than the **federal** government. He also believed that a truly democratic country should place power in the hands of its citizens. Little Mat learned about these ideas during long nights at the tavern.

Little Mat went to school in the poorly lit village schoolhouse and then briefly at the Kinderhook Academy. The schoolmaster was impressed with Mat's ability to read and write, but Mat left school before he was 14 years old. He planned to work as an **apprentice** under Francis Silvester, a local attorney, from 1796 until 1802. For the first year, Mat swept the floor, kept the fire burning, and copied **documents** by hand. He had more responsibilities by the time he was 15. The teenager had already begun to learn the legal profession. In fact, he had already argued his first case in front of a jury.

Within a few years, Martin Van Buren was ready for a change. He was interested in politics. Van Buren believed that average Americans, not just the wealthy, should express their opinions about government. The Silvester family thought differently. Van Buren became uncomfortable living with the Silvesters because he disagreed with their politics. So at age 18, he left the Silvesters. He began working to help Thomas Jefferson win the presidential election of 1800.

In Van Buren's time, many taverns functioned like inns. Travelers would stop at taverns for a warm meal or a place to sleep.

Below is a view of the Hudson River near West Point, south of Kinderhook. The Hudson River was a major transportation route in Van Buren's time.

Leaders in the Democratic-Republican Party noticed young Van Buren. He was elected to the congressional **caucus** in the city of Troy. Meanwhile, he continued his career as a lawyer, working for William P. Van Ness and finishing his law studies in 1803. Van

Buren then returned to Kinderhook where he opened his own law practice. He became one of the best-known lawyers in New York by defending the small farmers and shopkeepers of the area against rich landowners.

Like Van Buren, Hannah Hoes grew up in Kinderhook.

Shortly after opening his own law practice, Van Buren married his childhood sweetheart, Hannah Hoes. They wed on February 21, 1807, as soon as Van Buren felt he could support a family. Their marriage was a happy one, and Hannah was a loving and gentle person. They had six children before she died on February 5, 1819. Four of the children survived. Both of Van Buren's parents had died shortly before Hannah, so this was a sad time in his life. Van Buren never married again.

The name "Little Mat" stuck with Van Buren because he never grew taller than 5 feet, 6 inches. He was known in later years as "Little Van." He held himself upright and always dressed neatly in fine clothing. Whenever he could get away from his duties, he liked to fish and attend plays and operas. The twinkle in his eye, his cheerful optimism, and his quick, enthusiastic conversation made him popular.

Kinderhook was the model for the town in "The Legend of Sleepy Hollow," the story by Washington Irving about the Headless Horseman. In fact, Irving wrote the story while staying at Van Buren's home.

Van Buren may have been good at conversation, but he learned from his father to let others do the talking when it came to political subjects. Van Buren rarely took sides. Over the years, he developed a reputation for being **evasive** and shrewd. He had great **ambition,** but he also stuck by his principles, even when they made him unpopular.

Van Buren was the first president not of British descent.

COMING TO AMERICA

Cornelis Van Buurmalsen was a young farmer who lived near Amsterdam, the capital of the Netherlands. In 1631, he signed a **contract** with a man who owned land in the New Netherlands, a Dutch colony in what is now New York State. In the contract, Cornelis promised to farm the man's land in the New Netherlands for three years for about $92 in pay. In exchange, he would receive free transport to America.

Cornelis farmed the man's land for three years. Then, he returned to Amsterdam and signed another contract. This time, he received his own land to farm. He sailed back to America with his new wife and their son, who was born on the long ocean journey. They landed at New Amsterdam (now New York) on March 4, 1637, exactly 200 years before their great-great-great-grandson, Martin Van Buren, became the eighth president of the United States on March 4, 1837.

Cornelis was a good farmer. On October 24, 1646, he bought a large farm in Manhattan. His farm was located in what is today the bustling part of New York City called Greenwich Village. Their second son bought land in Kinderhook, which became the family home where Martin Van Buren grew up.

THE RED FOX OF KINDERHOOK

Martin Van Buren was working as a lawyer and raising his family when he began to pursue a political career. In 1809, he was named the chairman of the Democratic-Republican meetings in Albany, the capital of New York. By 1812, he had been elected to the state senate. He served as a state senator until 1820.

At the time, it was common to put people in jail if they owed money and could not pay it back. Van Buren worked to end this practice. He also supported the War of 1812 against Great Britain. The British navy had been stopping American ships and kidnapping American sailors. During the war, U.S. military forces needed more men. Van Buren proposed a **bill** to **draft** men into the army and navy.

Van Buren was called the Red Fox of Kinderhook, in part because of his bright red hair.

While a state senator, Van Buren also supported the building of the Erie Canal. The canal allowed goods to be shipped from the Atlantic Ocean to the Great Lakes of the Midwest. In this way, the canal helped open the American West to settlement.

The Democratic-Republican Party in New York was split into two groups. The members of one of these groups were followers of Governor DeWitt Clinton. Their rivals were called the Bucktails. Van Buren became the leader of the Bucktails, who helped him become the state attorney general in 1816.

In the early 1800s, the British sometimes captured American sailors and forced them to join the British navy. This practice, called impressment, was a leading cause of the War of 1812.

During this time, Van Buren helped rewrite New York's constitution. The changes doubled the number of people in the state who could vote. They also eliminated unnecessary state jobs.

As attorney general, Van Buren was the most important lawyer in the state of New York. But after three years, Governor Clinton removed him from this position. Van Buren and the Bucktails decided to challenge the governor. They formed a powerful group called the Albany Regency. These politicians won votes by using their political power to help people who voted for them.

This illustration shows men casting ballots in New York City. The New York Constitution of 1822 opened voting to more people. It gave the vote to some African Americans and to white men who did not own property.

14

During this time, people began to call Van Buren "the Little Magician" and "the Red Fox of Kinderhook." These names were given to him because of the sly, crafty way in which he achieved his goals.

In 1821, Van Buren was elected to the U.S. Senate. He immediately began working to reform voting laws. At that time, most states limited who could vote. Usually, only white men who owned land and paid taxes were allowed to cast ballots. Van Buren believed that all white men should be given the right to vote.

The next year, Van Buren suggested that Florida be admitted to the **Union,** which is another name for the United States. But there was a problem. Many people in Florida kept slaves. Most northerners didn't want

Van Buren's critics often compared him to animals. Some called him a fox. Others called him an opossum. Both comparisons imply he was sneaky.

In his first speech as a U.S. senator, Van Buren became so nervous that he suddenly stopped talking and sat down. After a few weeks, he regained his self-confidence. He eventually became a leader in the Senate.

another slave state in the Union. Southerners thought they should be able to decide for themselves whether to allow slavery. Van Buren came up with a way to give both sides part of what they wanted. He suggested that slave owners could keep any slaves who were already in Florida, but that no new slaves could be brought into the **territory.** It would be another two decades before Florida became a state, but politicians on both sides of the slavery issue liked Van Buren's ideas.

As a U.S. senator, Van Buren continued to follow the principles of Thomas Jefferson. Like Jefferson, Van Buren did not want a strong central government. He believed instead that the states should have more power. Like George Washington, Van Buren believed the United States should remain neutral in disputes between other countries. In 1826, President John Quincy Adams planned to send an American **representative** to a meeting called the Panama Congress. This meeting was intended to set up a united force of countries that would fight together against other unfriendly countries. Van Buren did not think the United States should attend the Panama Congress. He believed it went against the American policy of staying neutral.

Van Buren united the Democratic-Republicans in the various states. By so doing, he helped found the Democratic Party that is still a force in American politics. Van Buren was one of the first politicians to understand how to use political parties and operate them as "machines." He realized that political success depended on using newspapers and large meetings to spread the party's ideas to the many new voters in the country. He also realized that members of a party had to be well organized and loyal. "Political parties are inseparable from free government," Van Buren once said. "[They] are highly useful to the country." He believed that a strong, honest political party could keep one person from abusing power.

In 1828, Andrew Jackson was the Democratic Party's presidential **candidate.** Jackson was a war hero from the South. Van Buren supported Jackson and worked hard to help him win the presidency. Van

Van Buren's critics sometimes compared him to an opossum, which suggested that he was sneaky and evasive. Here, the "opossum" carries other politicians in his pouch.

17

The Whig Party was started to oppose President Andrew Jackson and the Democrats. Jackson's rivals thought he acted more like a king than a president. Because the British Whig Party opposed royalty in Great Britain, people who were against Jackson decided to call their political party the Whigs.

Buren helped create an image of Andrew Jackson as someone who cared about the common people. Van Buren also had a plan to convince many powerful Americans to vote for Jackson. He still controlled politics in New York through the Albany Regency, so he used the Regency to get himself elected governor of New York. As governor, Van Buren was better able to gather support to help elect Jackson president. New York backed Jackson, and Jackson won the presidency.

Less than three months later, Van Buren resigned. During his short time as governor, Van Buren had one important accomplishment. He sponsored the Safety

Martin Van Buren served as governor of New York for only three months. This portrait depicts him during this brief time. The capitol in Albany is visible in the background.

Fund Plan, which forced New York banks to set up a special fund to protect their customers. At that time, people lost all their savings if a bank went out of business. The money in the Safety Fund would be used to repay customers if a bank failed.

Van Buren resigned as governor because President Jackson asked him to become secretary of state. This meant he was in charge of U.S. relations with other countries. In 1830, Van Buren signed two **treaties.** The first was a treaty with Turkey that allowed the United States to sail the Black Sea. The second treaty was with Great Britain. It renewed trade with British territories in the West Indies.

In 1832, it was time for another presidential election. The Democratic Party again chose Jackson as its candidate. This time, Van Buren received the

The first **assassination** attempt on a U.S. president occurred on January 30, 1835. A housepainter named Richard Lawrence aimed two pistols at President Andrew Jackson in the Capitol. The pistols failed to fire. After that, Vice President Van Buren kept loaded pistols with him whenever he was in the Capitol.

Andrew Jackson's support helped Martin Van Buren win the presidency. This cartoon depicts Jackson (second from left) encouraging Van Buren (third from left) in his battle against William Henry Harrison, one of his Whig opponents.

nomination for vice president. During the **campaign,** Jackson and Van Buren promised to provide more opportunities for the common man. They won the election on December 5. Over the next four years, Van Buren supported Jackson on almost everything.

Jackson set Van Buren up to be the next president. Van Buren easily won the Democratic presidential nomination in 1836. Van Buren faced three opponents, all from the Whig Party. He won the election with ease.

SET-TO BETWEEN THE CHAMPION OLD TIP & THE SWELL DUTCHMAN OF KINDERHOOK—1836

THE PEGGY EATON AFFAIR

Martin Van Buren was President Andrew Jackson's closest adviser. Some other members of the president's **cabinet** grew jealous of Van Buren. They accused him of being sneaky and untrustworthy. Jackson, however, described Van Buren as "a true man."

Peggy Eaton was the new wife of the secretary of war, John Eaton (above). The other cabinet members and their wives treated Mrs. Eaton badly. They believed she was immoral. Rumors spread that she had lived with John Eaton before they were married. Jackson and Van Buren defended Mrs. Eaton, and tensions grew within the cabinet.

In the spring of 1831, Van Buren came up with an idea. If he and John Eaton resigned from their posts, Jackson could ask all the other cabinet members to leave, too. Jackson agreed to the plan.

Jackson appointed a new cabinet, and he rewarded Van Buren by naming him **minister** to Great Britain. The position did not last long, however. Van Buren returned to the United States in 1832 to run for vice president.

CHAPTER THREE

THE CAREFUL DUTCHMAN

Andrew Jackson's popularity helped Van Buren win the election of 1836. At his **inauguration** in 1837, Van Buren promised to "tread in the footsteps" of President Jackson. He also talked about the country's good fortune. He discussed how the "American

Martin Van Buren was elected president while serving as Andrew Jackson's vice president. Not until 1988 was another sitting vice president elected president.

Martin Van Buren taking the presidential oath of office on March 4, 1837. A few short weeks later, the country fell into a depression.

experiment" with democracy was setting an example for the rest of the world to follow.

Just a few weeks later, however, the Panic of 1837 set in. This would prove to be the worst **depression** the United States had experienced up to this time. It would set the tone for Van Buren's presidency.

The trouble started when President Jackson took all of the government's money out of the Second Bank of the United States, which was the national bank at the time. He placed the money in smaller state banks. These banks unwisely loaned money to people who wanted to buy land in the West. Many people bought land with the money they borrowed, hoping it would

As an adult, Martin Van Buren loved fine clothes. This probably grew from admiring the lawyers and politicians who stayed at his father's tavern. They wore hats on top of their white, powdered wigs. They wore colored coats with velvet pants and silk stockings. Their square-toed shoes sported silver buckles.

increase in value. If it did, they could sell the land for a profit and pay back their loans. This plan was risky. A great deal of land actually became less valuable in 1837, but people still had to pay back their loans. Because many people had no money to repay the banks, banks were forced to close.

Jackson tried to stop this abuse during his last months in office. He ordered that land be purchased only with gold or silver. Americans rushed to the banks to exchange their paper money for these precious metals. Unfortunately, the banks didn't have enough gold and silver to fill the demand. At the same time, three English banks failed. After this happened, other English banks wanted back any money they had loaned to American banks.

Many people blamed Andrew Jackson's stubbornness for the Panic of 1837. He is shown here on a donkey, an animal known for its stubbornness. The donkey would eventually become the symbol of the Democratic Party.

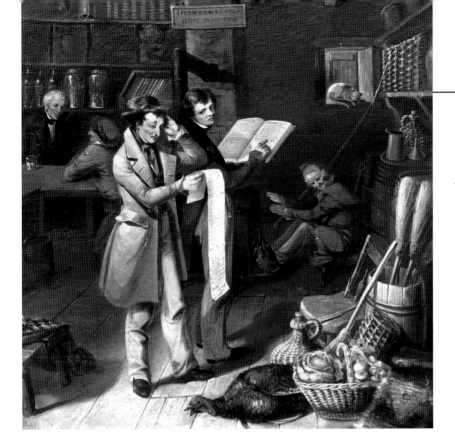

During the Panic of 1837, many Americans lost their jobs and had trouble feeding their families. Here, a man scratches his head at a long store bill listing the money he owes.

With no real money left, banks in Philadelphia and New York City closed on May 10, 1837, and the panic began. Hundreds of other banks and businesses failed. Thousands of people lost their homes, their land, and their jobs. Most of the factories on the East Coast closed. In some cities, people rioted for food. Eventually, nearly a thousand banks around the country failed.

Throughout this miserable time, Van Buren wore expensive clothes, such as soft leather gloves and coats with velvet collars. He rode around the streets of Washington in a luxurious horse-drawn coach driven by men in fancy uniforms. This made him unpopular with Americans, who thought he was behaving more like a king than an American president.

Some people called Martin Van Buren "Martin Van Ruin" because of the long depression during his presidency.

One of Van Buren's many nicknames, "the Little Magician," referred to both his small size and his cleverness. "It is said that he is a great magician," President Andrew Jackson once said. "I believe it, but his only wand is good common sense which he uses for the benefit of the country."

Van Buren continued Jackson's policies. He also worked to establish an independent **treasury** to deal with U.S. government money. He did not want state banks or another national bank looking after it. The treasury would make sure the national government did not spend more money than it had.

Many congressmen didn't like this idea because it would take money from banks in their home states. It was not until Van Buren's final year in office that Congress approved the treasury. Unfortunately, the depression had hurt many Americans. Some even starved or froze to death. Van Buren did nothing to help because he did not feel it was the government's job to help individuals. "The less government interferes with private pursuits the better," Van Buren said. His failure to handle the crisis caused him to lose popularity and the next election.

Van Buren's handling of Native American issues was not much better. In 1835, the government tried to force the Seminole Indians to leave Florida and move West, and the Second Seminole War began. This war was not popular with Americans. Over six years, it cost $20 million that could have been spent in better ways. The public also didn't like the way the Seminole leader, Osceola, was unfairly captured during a **truce.**

In 1838, Van Buren could have stopped the forced removal of 18,000 Cherokees, mostly from Georgia, to **reservations** west of the Mississippi. The Supreme Court said that the Native Americans had the right to remain on their lands, and most Americans did not support the removal. But Van Buren would not cancel Jackson's 1830 Indian Removal Act. Four thousand Cherokees died of cold, hunger, and disease traveling west on what became known as the Trail of Tears.

While Van Buren was slow to deal with problems at home, he did slightly better handling those with other countries. In 1837, Great Britain controlled Canada. A group of Canadian rebels attacked British soldiers there. The attack failed, and the rebels escaped to an island in the Niagara River along the border between the United States and Canada. Some Americans began to help the rebels. They sent supplies to them on the steamship *Caroline*. In December, Canadian troops working for the British captured the *Caroline* and set it on fire, killing an American.

In 1838, about 18,000 Cherokees were forced to leave their homes in the Southeast and move to what is now Oklahoma. More than 20 percent of them died during the thousand-mile march.

Martin Van Buren had been a widower for 18 years when he became president. After his eldest son, Abraham, married Angelica Singleton, she served as the White House hostess.

Martin Van Buren was the third president to be a widower when he moved into the White House.

Dolley Madison, the wife of former president James Madison, introduced Martin Van Buren's eldest son, Abraham, to Angelica Singleton. About 18 months after Van Buren's inauguration, the couple was married. Abraham served as President Van Buren's private secretary, and Angelica acted as White House hostess.

Van Buren was angered by the attack, but he was also unhappy that Americans had ignored the U.S. policy of remaining neutral. He believed the Americans should not have helped the Canadian rebels. Although Congress wanted him to declare war on Great Britain, Van Buren refused. He insisted that America must remain neutral. He sent an army to the Canadian border, hoping to calm the situation and avoid war. The rebels gave up on January 13.

The following year, fighting broke out between Canada and the United States in what became known as the Aroostook War. Lumberjacks fought over who owned the trees in the Aroostook Valley on the border between the state of Maine and New Brunswick, Canada. Van Buren continued his policy of neutrality. He sent General Winfield Scott to stop the fighting and negotiate a peace treaty, which was signed on March 25, 1839.

That same year, another crisis arose. A Spanish ship named *La Amistad* was transporting slaves from Africa. The enslaved Africans seized the ship, hoping to win their freedom. They ended up in Connecticut, and American leaders had to decide what to do with them. The Spanish ambassador demanded that the ship and the Africans be returned to the Spanish. Van Buren agreed, mostly because he didn't want to anger his southern supporters, who favored slavery.

But Van Buren's stance enraged those Americans who opposed slavery. Finally, a U.S. court ordered that the slaves from *La Amistad* be freed and returned to their homeland.

Washington, D.C., was a large swamp with open sewers and pigs roaming the street during Van Buren's time.

Enslaved Africans took over a ship called La Amistad *in June 1839. They were eventually freed. They returned to their home in what is now Nigeria in 1841.*

THE SECOND BANK OF THE UNITED STATES

In 1816, a **charter** gave the Second Bank of the United States the right to handle the country's money for the next 20 years. This bank was not run by the government. Instead, it was owned by 200 of the richest men in America along with some foreigners. The bank had the power to print money whenever it wanted. It controlled how much money was available. This gave the bank great power over the United States government and its citizens. The bank's charter would expire in 1836. That meant Congress had to decide whether to keep the Second Bank open. The bank's president, Nicholas Biddle, paid many congressmen, businessmen, and members of the press so they would help keep the bank in business.

Andrew Jackson and Martin Van Buren believed the bank helped only the rich. They thought that it should help all Americans instead. In 1833, Jackson took the government's money out of the Second Bank. This led to the Panic of 1837. But Van Buren and Jackson finally had their way when the bank was closed in 1836. The picture below depicts Jackson attacking the monster bank.

★★★★★★★★★★★★★★★★★★★★★★★★★★★

CHAPTER FOUR

STANDING FIRM

Martin Van Buren lost popularity over the four years he was president. The Panic of 1837 was a major reason for this, but the Trail of Tears and the Seminole War also hurt him. Nonetheless, the Democrats again chose him to be their presidential candidate in 1840. The election became known as the "hard cider campaign." Van Buren's opponents, the Whigs, insisted that he was so much like a king, he would rather drink French wine than American hard cider, an alcoholic drink.

The Whigs paraded their candidate, William Henry Harrison, around the country. They held events with music and free hard cider for people to drink. They claimed that Harrison was a man of the people. Harrison crushed Van Buren in the election. Van Buren had been beaten using the same techniques

Martin Van Buren in 1857

he had invented to get Jackson elected president. His opponents had promoted a candidate who appealed to the common man. "Van, Van, is a used up man," the Whigs chanted.

Van Buren ran twice more for president, but he failed both times. When he attended the Democratic Party **convention** in 1844, he had the support of the majority of the party. But then he refused to support the **annexation** of Texas. The **Republic** of Texas had gained its independence from Mexico in 1836. Now it wanted to be accepted into the United States. Even though many Americans approved, Van Buren did not. Allowing Texas into the Union would have added

William Henry Harrison's supporters claimed that he was a common man who had grown up in a log cabin and liked to drink hard cider. This cartoon shows Harrison's hard cider and log cabin train knocking over Van Buren's carriage.

another slave state. It would also have resulted in a war with Mexico. Because Van Buren stood firm on his principles, he lost the nomination. James Polk was nominated instead. Polk went on to become president. During his time in office, he annexed Texas and slavery spread.

Van Buren became more opposed to slavery over time. In 1948, he was nominated as a candidate for president by the Free Soil Party. This group was devoted to opposing slavery. Van Buren came in third and retired from politics. The 1850 census described him as a "farmer," but he was regarded by many as an **elder statesman.**

In 1852, Van Buren traveled to Europe, where he lived for two years. He was the first ex-president to

Van Buren's son John followed in his footsteps. He was a member of U.S. Congress from 1841 to 1843.

Martin Van Buren lived in his Lindenwald mansion in Kinderhook from 1839 until his death in 1862. The 36-room house is now a national historic site.

leave the United States. In Italy, he began writing his life story, in which he discussed his lifelong ambition to win the presidency.

Van Buren returned to the United States and settled down. His home, called Lindenwald, was a large, two-story brick house in Kinderhook. The Van Ness family, friends of the Van Burens, had built the house back in 1797. By 1824, they could no longer afford it. Martin Van Buren paid $14,000 for the house and the surrounding land in 1839. He turned it into a working farm. Over the years, he expanded the house and made it more beautiful. He also installed modern conveniences, such as ranges in the kitchen, running water, a bath, and a water heater.

Although Van Buren never again held public office, he still took an interest in politics. He supported both Franklin Pierce and Abraham Lincoln when they ran for president.

On July 24, 1862, Van Buren died of asthma. The funeral procession to the cemetery included 81 carriages carrying people who had come to pay their last respects. Van Buren was buried beside his wife and parents.

Each December 5, the day Martin Van Buren was born, a ceremony is held at a local church in honor of a man who set high goals and reached them. Van Buren

Some people believe the word "OK" became popular during Martin Van Buren's reelection campaign in 1840. "OK" was used to refer to Van Buren's home-town, Kinderhook, which was called "Old Kinderhook" in speeches and print. O.K. clubs were soon formed to support Van Buren's campaign, and "OK" soon came to mean "all right."

Martin Van Buren's grave is in the Kinderhook Reformed Church cemetery.

was an enthusiastic and clever politician. Unfortunately, he was not able to help the country when it truly needed a leader. Van Buren is not remembered as a great president, but he was willing to stand by his principles—even when they made him unpopular.

From childhood, Martin Van Buren loved politics. Throughout his lifetime, he was the most powerful person in New York politics. He helped found the Democratic Party and helped reshape U.S. government. He believed the voice of the people should be heard.

Martin Van Buren had a successful political career but a difficult presidency. He once said that the two happiest days of his life were the day he became president and the day he left the presidency.

That's you Dad! more
"FREE SOIL."
We'll rat'em out yet.
Long life to
Davy Wilmot.

VAN BUREN'S VIEW OF SLAVERY

Slavery was still allowed in New York when Martin Van Buren was born, and his father owned six slaves. Van Buren himself owned one slave, a man named Tom. In 1814, Tom ran away. Van Buren made no effort to find him. Ten years later, Van Buren learned that Tom was living in Massachusetts. Van Buren agreed to sell Tom as long as he could be captured "without violence."

While in office, Van Buren was caught between the southern states, which allowed slavery, and the northern states, which preferred to end slavery. Only a **compromise** would keep the Union together, and he found one. He believed the government should let slavery continue where it already existed but not allow it to spread.

In his later years, Van Buren opposed slavery completely. In 1843, he and his son John led the Barnburners, a group within the Democratic Party that fought against slavery. Their critics thought they were too unwilling to compromise. They called them "Barnburners" after a story about a farmer who burned down his barn to get rid of the rats. The cartoon above shows Martin and John Van Buren burning down a barn. Because other Democrats would not agree with them about slavery, the Barnburners left the Democratic Party in 1848 and formed the Free Soil Party. On August 9, 1848, the Free Soilers nominated Van Buren for president. He would not to return to the White House, however. A southern slave owner and military hero named Zachary Taylor won the election and became president.

1780	1800	1810	1820	1830

1782
Martin Van Buren is born in Kinderhook, New York, on December 5.

1801
Van Buren is elected representative to the Democratic-Republican Party caucus in Troy, New York.

1803
Van Buren begins to practice law.

1807
Van Buren marries his childhood sweetheart, Hannah Hoes, on February 21.

1812
Van Buren is elected a state senator. He becomes the leader of the Jeffersonian Democratic-Republicans in New York. During the War of 1812, he proposes a bill to begin drafting men into the military.

1816
Van Buren is named the attorney general of New York.

1819
Hannah Hoes Van Buren dies of tuberculosis. New York governor DeWitt Clinton removes Van Buren from his position as attorney general. Van Buren helps establish the Albany Regency, a powerful political group, to oppose Clinton.

1821
Van Buren is elected a U.S. senator.

1826
Van Buren discourages President John Quincy Adams's attempt to send representatives to the Panama Congress, believing that it goes against the nation's policy of neutrality.

1828
Van Buren manages Andrew Jackson's presidential campaign. With the help of the Albany Regency, Van Buren is elected governor of New York.

1829
Van Buren is governor of New York for 71 days before Jackson names him the secretary of state.

1831
Van Buren resigns from Jackson's cabinet when other members mistreat Peggy Eaton, wife of Secretary of War John Eaton. Afterward, Jackson names Van Buren minister to Great Britain.

1832
The Democratic Party nominates Van Buren as Jackson's vice presidential running mate. Jackson and Van Buren win the election in December.

1833
President Jackson pulls government money out of the Second Bank of the United States and puts it into smaller state banks. This leads to speculation on land in the West and eventually to a severe depression.

1834
The Whig Party is formed to oppose the Democratic Party.

1836
Jackson orders that land be purchased only with gold or silver, not with paper money. Americans rush to banks to exchange paper money for precious metals. Jackson supports Martin Van Buren as the Democratic presidential candidate. Van Buren is elected the eighth president of the United States.

1837
The Panic of 1837 begins when banks stop converting paper money to silver and gold.

1838
Eighteen thousand Cherokees are forced from their homes as part of the Indian Removal Act. Four thousand of them die along the Trail of Tears. The Aroostook War over the boundary between United States and Canada begins.

1839
Van Buren orders that the enslaved Africans who had seized the Spanish ship *La Amistad* be returned to their Spanish owners. A federal court later decides to free the Africans.

1840
Van Buren signs a bill creating an independent treasury in an attempt to make the nation more financially stable. William Henry Harrison defeats Van Buren in the presidential election.

1844
Van Buren loses the Democratic presidential nomination to James K. Polk.

1848
Van Buren is the presidential candidate of the Free Soil Party. He loses to Zachary Taylor, a southern slaveholder. Van Buren retires from political life.

1852
Van Buren travels to Europe, becoming the first president to go abroad after his term.

1862
Van Buren dies at his Lindenwald estate on July 24.

GLOSSARY

ambition (am-BISH-un) Ambition is a strong desire to succeed. Van Buren had ambition to do well in politics.

annexation (an-ek-SAY-shun) Annexation is the joining of something smaller (such as a territory) to something bigger (such as a country). Van Buren was against the annexation of Texas.

apprentice (uh-PREN-tiss) An apprentice is a person who is learning a skill under the teaching of an expert. At age 14, Van Buren worked as an apprentice to an attorney in order to learn about the law.

assassination (uh-sass-ih-NAY-shun) An assassination is when someone is murdered, especially a well-known person. In 1835, an assassination attempt was made on Andrew Jackson's life.

bill (BILL) A bill is an idea for a new law that is presented to a group of lawmakers. Van Buren proposed a bill to draft men into the military.

cabinet (KAB-nit) A cabinet is the group of people who advise a president. President Jackson offered Van Buren a position in his cabinet.

campaign (kam-PAYN) A campaign is the process of running for an election, including activities such as giving speeches or attending rallies. During their campaign, Jackson and Van Buren promised more opportunities to common people.

candidate (KAN-duh-det) A candidate is a person running in an election. Several candidates run for president every four years.

caucus (KAW-kus) A caucus is a meeting of a political group to make plans, choose candidates, and decide how to vote. Van Buren attended his first caucus in 1801.

charter (CHAR-tur) A charter is when the government gives a person or group a special right. In 1816, a charter gave the Second Bank of the United States the right to handle the country's money for the next 20 years.

compromise (KOM-pruh-myz) A compromise is a way to settle a disagreement in which both sides give up part of what they want. Van Buren tried to keep the country united by making the leaders of the North and the South reach a compromise.

contract (KAWN-trakt) A contract is a legal agreement between two or more people. Cornelis Van Buurmalsen signed a contract agreeing to farm land in exchange for transport to America.

convention (kun-VEN-shun) A convention is a meeting. Political parties hold national conventions every four years to choose their presidential candidates.

depression (deh-PRESH-un) A depression is a period of time in which there is little business activity and many people are out of work. The Panic of 1837 started a depression.

documents (DOK-yuh-ments) Documents are papers with important information. Van Buren copied documents by hand when he was a lawyer's apprentice.

draft (DRAFT) When the government drafts people, it makes them join the military as soldiers. Van Buren proposed a bill to draft men into the army and navy.

elder statesman (EL-dur STAYTZ-man) An elder statesman is an older politician who has left office and is still asked for advice. Van Buren was an elder statesman until he died.

evasive (ee-VAY-sive) If people are evasive, they avoid answering questions about their opinions. Van Buren had a reputation for being evasive.

federal (FED-ur-ul) Federal means having to do with the central government of the United States, rather than the government of a state or city. Thomas Jefferson believed the states should have more power than the federal government.

inauguration (ih-naw-gyuh-RAY-shun) An inauguration is the ceremony that takes place when a new president begins a term. Van Buren spoke of the nation's good fortune at his inauguration.

minister (MIN-uh-stur) A minister is a person who represents one country in another country. Van Buren was briefly the minister to Great Britain.

neutral (NOO-trul) If people are neutral, they do not take sides. Van Buren believed the United States should be neutral and not take sides in problems that arose among other nations.

nomination (nom-uh-NAY-shun) If someone receives a nomination, he or she is chosen by a political party to run for an office, such as the presidency. Van Buren received the Democratic nomination for vice president.

political party (puh-LIT-uh-kul PAR-tee) A political party is a group of people who share similar ideas about how to run a government. Martin Van Buren helped found the Democratic Party.

politics (PAWL-uh-tiks) Politics refers to the actions and practices of the government. Politicians and lawyers visited Abraham Van Buren's tavern to discuss politics.

polling place (POH-ling PLAYSS) A polling place is a public building where people go to vote. The town of Kinderhook used Abraham Van Buren's tavern as a polling place.

principles (PRIN-suh-puls) Principles are people's basic beliefs, or what they believe to be right and true. When Van Buren stood by his principles, he did what he felt was right.

representative (rep-ree-ZEN-tuh-tiv) A representative is someone who attends a meeting, having agreed to speak or act for others. President John Quincy Adams wanted to send a U.S. representative to the Panama Congress in 1826.

republic (ree-PUB-lik) A republic is a nation in which citizens elect representatives to their government. Texas became a republic when it won independence from Mexico.

reservations (rez-ur-VAY-shunz) Reservations are parcels of land set aside for Native Americans by the U.S. government. Native Americans were forced to leave their land and live on reservations.

territory (TAYR-ih-tor-ee) A territory is land or a region, especially land that belongs to a government. Northerners did not want slavery allowed in new territories such as Florida.

treasury (TREZH-ur-ee) A treasury manages a government's or an organization's money. Van Buren set up an independent treasury to handle the country's money.

treaties (TREE-teez) Treaties are formal agreements made between nations. Van Buren signed treaties with Turkey and Great Britain in 1830.

truce (TROOS) A truce is when two sides in a war agree to stop fighting for a period of time. American soldiers unfairly captured Osceola during a truce.

union (YOON-yen) A union is the joining together of two or more people or groups of people, such as states. The United States is also known as the Union.

THE UNITED STATES GOVERNMENT

The United States government is divided into three equal branches: the executive, the legislative, and the judicial. This division helps prevent abuses of power because each branch has to answer to the other two. No one branch can become too powerful.

EXECUTIVE BRANCH

PRESIDENT
VICE PRESIDENT
DEPARTMENTS

The job of the executive branch is to enforce the laws. It is headed by the president, who serves as the spokesperson for the United States around the world. The president signs bills into law and appoints important officials such as federal judges. He or she is also the commander in chief of the U.S. military. The president is assisted by the vice president, who takes over if the president dies or cannot carry out the duties of the office.

The executive branch also includes various departments, each focused on a specific topic. They include the Defense Department, the Justice Department, and the Agriculture Department. The department heads, along with other officials such as the vice president, serve as the president's closest advisers, called the cabinet.

LEGISLATIVE BRANCH

CONGRESS
Senate and
House of Representatives

The job of the legislative branch is to make the laws. It consists of Congress, which is divided into two parts: the Senate and the House of Representatives. The Senate has 100 members, and the House of Representatives has 435 members. Each state has two senators. The number of representatives a state has varies depending on the state's population.

Besides making laws, Congress also passes budgets and enacts taxes. In addition, it is responsible for declaring war, maintaining the military, and regulating trade with other countries.

JUDICIAL BRANCH

SUPREME COURT
COURTS OF APPEALS
DISTRICT COURTS

The job of the judicial branch is to interpret the laws. It consists of the nation's federal courts. Trials are held in district courts. During trials, judges must decide what laws mean and how they apply. Courts of appeals review the decisions made in district courts.

The nation's highest court is the Supreme Court. If someone disagrees with a court of appeals ruling, he or she can ask the Supreme Court to review it. The Supreme Court may refuse. The Supreme Court makes sure that decisions and laws do not violate the Constitution.

CHOOSING
THE PRESIDENT

I t may seem odd, but American voters don't elect the president directly. Instead, the president is chosen using what is called the Electoral College.

Each state gets as many votes in the Electoral College as its combined total of senators and representatives in Congress. For example, Iowa has two senators and five representatives, so it gets seven electoral votes. Although the District of Columbia does not have any voting members in Congress, it gets three electoral votes. Usually, the candidate who wins the most votes in any given state receives all of that state's electoral votes.

To become president, a candidate must get more than half of the Electoral College votes. There are a total of 538 votes in the Electoral College, so a candidate needs 270 votes to win. If nobody receives 270 Electoral College votes, the House of Representatives chooses the president.

With the Electoral College system, the person who receives the most votes nationwide does not always receive the most electoral votes. This happened most recently in 2000, when Al Gore received half a million more national votes than George W. Bush. Bush became president because he had more Electoral College votes.

THE WHITE HOUSE

The White House is the official home of the president of the United States. It is located at 1600 Pennsylvania Avenue NW in Washington, D.C. In 1792, a contest was held to select the architect who would design the president's home. James Hoban won. Construction took eight years.

The first president, George Washington, never lived in the White House. The second president, John Adams, moved into the house in 1800, though the inside was not yet complete. During the War of 1812, British soldiers burned down much of the White House. It was rebuilt several years later.

The White House was changed through the years. Porches were added, and President Theodore Roosevelt added the West Wing. President William Taft changed the shape of the presidential office, making it into the famous Oval Office. While Harry Truman was president, the old house was discovered to be structurally weak. All the walls were reinforced with steel, and the rooms were rebuilt.

Today, the White House has 132 rooms (including 35 bathrooms), 28 fireplaces, and 3 elevators. It takes 570 gallons of paint to cover the outside of the six-story building. The White House provides the president with many ways to relax. It includes a putting green, a jogging track, a swimming pool, a tennis court, and beautifully landscaped gardens. The White House also has a movie theater, a billiard room, and a one-lane bowling alley.

PRESIDENTIAL PERKS

The job of president of the United States is challenging. It is probably one of the most stressful jobs in the world. Because of this, presidents are paid well, though not nearly as well as the leaders of large corporations. In 2007, the president earned $400,000 a year. Presidents also receive extra benefits that make the demanding job a little more appealing.

★ **Camp David:** In the 1940s, President Franklin D. Roosevelt chose this heavily wooded spot in the mountains of Maryland to be the presidential retreat, where presidents can relax. Even though it is a retreat, world business is conducted there. Most famously, President Jimmy Carter met with Middle Eastern leaders at Camp David in 1978. The result was a peace agreement between Israel and Egypt.

★ *Air Force One*: The president flies on a jet called *Air Force One*. It is a Boeing 747-200B that has been modified to meet the president's needs.

Air Force One is the size of a large home. It is equipped with a dining room, sleeping quarters, a conference room, and office space. It also has two kitchens that can provide food for up to 50 people.

★ **The Secret Service:** While not the most glamorous of the president's perks, the Secret Service is one of the most important. The Secret Service is a group of highly trained agents who protect the president and the president's family.

★ **The Presidential State Car:** The presidential limousine is a stretch Cadillac DTS.

It has been armored to protect the president in case of attack. Inside the plush car are a foldaway desk, an entertainment center, and a communications console.

★ **The Food:** The White House has five chefs who will make any food the president wants. The White House also has an extensive wine collection.

★ **Retirement:** A former president receives a pension, or retirement pay, of just under $180,000 a year. Former presidents also receive Secret Service protection for the rest of their lives.

FACTS

QUALIFICATIONS

To run for president, a candidate must

- ★ be at least 35 years old
- ★ be a citizen who was born in the United States
- ★ have lived in the United States for 14 years

TERM OF OFFICE

A president's term of office is four years.
No president can stay in office for more than two terms.

ELECTION DATE

The presidential election takes place every four years on the first Tuesday of November.

INAUGURATION DATE

Presidents are inaugurated on January 20.

OATH OF OFFICE

I do solemnly swear I will faithfully execute the office of the President of the United States and will to the best of my ability preserve, protect, and defend the Constitution of the United States.

WRITE A LETTER TO THE PRESIDENT

One of the best things about being a U.S. citizen is that Americans get to participate in their government. They can speak out if they feel government leaders aren't doing their jobs. They can also praise leaders who are going the extra mile. Do you have something you'd like the president to do? Should the president worry more about the environment and encourage people to recycle? Should the government spend more money on our schools? You can write a letter to the president to say how you feel!

1600 Pennsylvania Avenue
Washington, D.C. 20500
You can even send an e-mail to: president@whitehouse.gov

BOOKS

Chambers, Veronica. *Amistad Rising: A Story of Freedom.* Austin, TX: Raintree/Steck-Vaughn, 1998.

Collier, Christopher, and James Lincoln. *Andrew Jackson's America.* New York: Marshall Cavendish, 1999.

Cornelissen, Cornelia. *Soft Rain: A Story of the Cherokee Trail of Tears.* New York: Delacorte Press, 1998.

Creative Media Applications. *American Presidents in World History.* Westport, CT: Greenwood Press, 2003.

Doak, Robin S. *Profiles of the Presidents: Martin Van Buren.* Minneapolis, MN: Compass Point Books, 2003.

Favor, Lesli J. *Martin Van Buren, America's 8th President.* New York: Children's Press, 2003.

Gibson, Karen Bush. *New Netherland: The Dutch Settle the Hudson Valley.* Hockessin, DE: Mitchell Lane Publishers, 2007.

VIDEOS

The History Channel Presents The Presidents. DVD (New York: A&E Home Video, 2005).

National Geographic's Inside the White House. DVD (Washington, DC: National Geographic Video, 2003).

INTERNET SITES

Visit our Web page for lots of links about Martin Van Buren and other U.S. presidents:

http://www.childsworld.com/links

Note to Parents, Teachers, and Librarians: We routinely verify our Web links to make sure they are safe, active sites—so encourage your readers to check them out!

INDEX

Adams, John Quincy, 16, 38
Albany Regency, 14, 18, 38
Amistad, La, 29, 39
Aroostook War, 29, 39

Barnburners, 33, 37
Biddle, Nicholas, 30
Bucktails, 13, 14, 15

Canada, 27, 29, 39
Canadian rebels, 27–28, 37
Caroline, 27
Cherokees, 26–27, 28, 39
Clinton, DeWitt, 13, 14, 15, 38

Democratic Party, 16–17, 19, 20, 31, 32, 38, 39
Democratic-Republican Party, 5, 8, 12, 13, 16, 38
depression, 23–25, 38
draft (military), 12, 38

Eaton, John, 21, 38
Eaton, Peggy, 21, 38
Erie Canal, 13

federal government, 6, 16, 26
Florida, 15–16
Free Soil Party, 33, 37, 39

Great Britain, 12–13, 19, 21, 27–28

Harrison, William Henry, 20, 31–32, 39
Hoes, Hannah. *See* Van Buren, Hannah

Independent Treasury Act, 37
Indian Removal Act, 27, 28, 39
Irving, Washington, 9

Jackson, Andrew, 17–24, 26, 27, 30, 32, 38, 39
Jefferson, Thomas, 5, 6, 7, 16, 36

Kinderhook, 4–5, 6, 9, 11, 17, 34, 35, 36, 38

"Legend of Sleepy Hollow, The" (Irving), 9
Lincoln, Abraham, 35
Lindenwald, 34, 39

Madison, Dolley 28
Mexico, 32–33

Native Americans, 26–27

Osceola, leaders of the Seminoles, 26

Panama Congress, 16, 38
Panic of 1837, 23–25, 30, 31, 38, 39
Pierce, Franklin, 35
political parties, 16–17, 18, 39
Polk, James, 33, 39

Scott, Winfield, 29
Second Bank of the United States, 23, 30, 38
Second Seminole War, 26, 30, 31
Seminole Indians, 26
Silvester, Francis, 6–7
slavery, 6, 15–16, 29, 32–33, 37, 39

Taylor, Zachary, 37, 39
Texas, annexation of, 32–33
Trail of Tears, 27, 31, 39
treasury, 26, 39

Van Buren, Abraham (father), 4, 5–6, 25
Van Buren, Abraham (son), 26
Van Buren, Angelica, 26
Van Buren, Hannah, 9, 38
Van Buren, John, 33, 37
Van Buren, Maria, 4
Van Buren, Martin
    apprenticeship of, 6–7
    as attorney general of New York, 13–14, 38
    birth of, 4, 38
    death of, 35, 39
    election as president, 20, 39
    as governor of New York, 18–19, 20, 38
    inauguration of, 22–23
    international travel of, 33–34, 39
    law career of, 7, 8–9, 12, 38
    marriage of, 9, 38
    as minister to Great Britain, 21, 38
    nicknames of, 9, 12, 15, 22, 25, 26
    opposition to slavery, 32–33, 37
    presidency of, 22–31, 39
    reputation of, 9–10, 15, 16, 17, 25
    as secretary of state, 19, 21, 38
    as state senator, 12–13, 38
    support of common people, 9, 12, 18, 19, 30, 31, 36
    as U.S. senator, 15–16, 38
    as vice president, 20, 38
Van Ness, William P., 8
voting laws, 14, 15

War of 1812, 12–13, 15, 38
Washington, George, 16
Whig Party, 18, 20, 31–32, 39